LEAD ME TO SUCCESS IN PUBLISHING: 101 WAYS

LEAD ME TO SUCCESS IN PUBLISHING

101 WAYS

Melissa G Wilson and Jon Malysiak

networlding
PUBLISHING

Lead Me to Success in Publishing: 101 Ways
By Melissa G Wilson and Jon Malysiak

ISBN 978-0-9838128-6-9

Copyright Networlding Publishing
All Rights Reserved

Chicago, IL
www.networlding.com

TABLE OF CONTENTS

1 INTRODUCTION — 1

Things are Different 3

2 BLOGS — 5

Why Blog? 6

Tip #1: Figure Out Your Blog Idea 6

Tip #2: Choose a Memorable Name or
Catch Phrase 7

Tip #3: Start a Blog (or Restart Your Blog) 8

Tip #4: Get Writing.. 9

How to Blog Effectively 11

Tip #5: Interact with Your Audience 11

Tip #6: Encourage Sharing................................. 12

Tip #7: Be Yourself... 13

Using Your Blog as a Starting Point for Publishing 14

Tip #8: Build Your Brand................................... 14

Tip #9: Mention Your Grand Book Idea 15

Tip #10: Offer Free Sections of Your Book Through Your Blog.. 16

Tip #11: Share Your Book News ONLY on Your Blog.. 17

The Personal Blogging Experience (Now with Video!)........... 18

Tip #12: Add Video Blogs................................... 18

Tip #13: Address Reader Questions 19

Tip #14: Talk about Your Personal Life (to Connect!) 20

Tip #15: Don't Make It All About Your Book 21

3 BOOKS — 23

To Book or Not to Book? 24

Tip #16: Find a Unique Idea… 24

Tip #17: Take a New Look at an Old Idea 26

Tip #18: Use What You Teach and Know Well 26

Tip #19: Niche Research 27

Types of Books to Create 29

Tip #20: Think about Series 29

Tip #21: Complementary Book Ideas 30

Tip #22: Don't Limit Yourself to Books 31

Making Money with eBooks 33

Tip #23: Give Something Away 33

Tip #24: Sell a Part/Sample Chapter 34

Tip #25: Think about Different Supplementary Products 35

4 SOCIAL MEDIA — 37

Facebook — 38

- Tip #26: Get an Author/Business Page — 38
- Tip #27: Be Active — 38
- Tip #28: Answer Your Messages — 39
- Tip #29: Advertise — 39

Twitter — 41

- Tip #30: Check in Frequently — 41
- Tip #31: Get the Right Followers — 42
- Tip #32: Interact with Others — 42
- Tip #33: Retweet, Retweet — 43
- Tip #34: Don't Just Schedule Your Tweets — 43

LinkedIn — 45

- Tip #35: Set up Your Profile — 45
- Tip #36: Get Involved in Groups — 46
- Tip #37: Connect! — 46
- Tip #38: Start a Group — 47
- Tip #39: Update Often — 47
- Tip #40: Look for New Contacts Often — 48

Other Social Media Options 49

Tip #41: Google+ 49

Tip #42: Tumblr 50

Tip #43: Hub Pages 50

Tip #44: Pinterest 51

Tip #45: Twaitter 51

Tip #46: Hootsuite 52

Tip #47: Tweetdeck 52

Tip #48: Posterous 52

Tip #49: Ning 53

Social Media Advice 54

Tip #50: How Often 54

Tip #51: What to Say 55

Tip #52: Cross Posting 55

Tip #53: To Schedule or Not to Schedule? 56

Tip #54: How to Keep Up with Posts 57

Tip #55: Time to Get Help? 58

5 MORE ADVICE — 59

Guidebooks 60

Tip #56: How to Guide 60

Tip #57: What to Guide 61

Tip #58: How to Create Guidebooks 62

Tip #59: Pictures and Videos 62

Tip #60: When to Guide 63

Video Training 64

Tip #61: Brainstorm Videos 64

Tip #62: The Equipment You Need 65

Tip #63: Training Formats/Products 65

Tip #64: Length of Training 66

Tip #65: Training Packages 67

Tip #66: Create High Quality Videos 68

The Truth about Book Design 69

Tip #67: Organize Your Book 69

Tip #68: Book Layouts 70

Tip #69: Design Software 71

Tip #70: Professional or On Your Own? 72

Tip #71: Design Really Matters 72

Tip #72: Save Design for Last? 73

Hybrid Publishing 75

Tip #73: Why Hybrid Works 75

Tip #74: Get Editing Help 76

Tip #75: Get Design Help 77

Tip #76: Get Writing Help 77

Tip #77: Do You Need an Agent? 78

Tip #78: Self Publishing Works 79

Tip #79: Be Your Own Agent 79

More Publishing Tips 81

Tip #80: Write Guest Blogs 81

Tip #81: Teach Classes 81

Tip #82: Give Speeches 82

Tip #83: Pricing Right 82

Tip #84: Marketing Materials 83

Tip #85: Translate Your Words 84

Tip #86: Don't Forget About Fiction 85

Tip #87: Blog Relationships 85

Tip #88: Do Some Good 86

Tip #89: Team Up with Others 86

Tip #90: Get a Website started 87

Tip #91: Have a release party 88

Tip #92: Talk to Local Booksellers 88

Tip #93: The Right Bio 89

Tip #94: Your Press Packet 89

Tip #95: Send Out Sample Copies 90

Tip #96: Get Testimonials...NOW! 91

Tip #97: Edit, Edit, Edit 91

Tip #98: Edit Again 91

Tip #99: Thoughts about Ghostwriters 92

Tip #100: Planning Your NExt Book 93
Tip #101: Get Started Now! 93

6 CONCLUSION — 95

APPENDIX — 97

Top Ten Mistakes Authors Commonly Make 97

Mistake #1: Assume That Your Work Is Done Once You've Turned in the Final Draft of the Manuscript 98

Mistake #2: Assume That Because an Experience is Meaningful to You, It is Going to Be Meaningful to Charlie and His Aunt…Because It Won't Be 99

Mistake #3: Assume That Your Book is for Everyone 101

Mistake #4: Try to Publish Without an Agent .. 102

Mistake #5: Become Too Attached to a Title 105

Mistake #6: Ignore Deadlines 106

Mistake #7: Ignore an Agent's Submission Guidelines 108

Mistake #8: Assume that the Author Advance is an Indication of a Publisher's Commitment to Your Book 111

Mistake #9: Act Like a Diva 114

Mistake #10: Beat Yourself Up if Your Book Doesn't Sell to Your Expectations 115

AUTHOR BIOS — 117

INTRODUCTION

The world of publishing is changing, and you've already begun to realize it. While there are still the same authors on the same tables at your local bookstore, there are other names that are showing up online and in your email box.

But how are they getting attention if they're not doing publishing 'the way it's always been done'?

For a thought leader like you, you already have bigger ideas about how the world should, rather, how the world COULD work to support the cutting edge thoughts you want to share. You're not interested in simply doing the same old things because you're not interested in the same old results.

In the past year, you've noticed how social media has changed the way we interact and the way we share information. You've seen Facebook turn into a sort of gathering place and Twitter become the first place where thoughts are born.

But you want to publish. You want to take your ideas a step further and you're not interested in spending a lot of money or sending out hundreds of proposals.

Welcome to 2012. This is YOUR year of success.

THINGS ARE DIFFERENT

It's no surprise that publishing is changing. With the explosion of e-readers, people are turning to digital platforms to find the information they want, the information they crave.

While paperback books and hardbacks are still beloved friends, you can see the publishing world shifting when you see even the biggest bookstores starting to shut their doors.

Ideas need a new place to call home, and that home is online and with other forms of publishing.

By publishing on your own (and don't think it's just about creating a book), you can:

- Spend less
- Make more
- Create different products
- Spread the word more easily
- Have control over your ideas
- Generate a following

The new world of publishing is changing the way that people access information, but it's also changing the choices you have as a thought leader.

You don't need to settle for anything less than everything you want...while still being a leader and innovator.

You don't have to follow the 'old' rules of publishing, but you do need to know the 'new' rules are to lead you to success in publishing.

BLOGS
2

Right when you thought that blogs were dead, a new wave of voices started to swell up from the waves of the ocean that is the Internet. Suddenly, the Seth Godins of the Web were making a difference because they had a regular way to connect with their readers.

And with their book audience.

Before you have a book, you can blog. And that blog can turn into a way to help your book idea turn into reality.

WHY BLOG?

The blog is a place where your thoughts come to be assembled and delivered to your audience. This content is updated regularly (hopefully) and it creates a conversation with the readers, one that they can join in the comments or by sharing on social media networks.

But we're getting ahead of ourselves.

Tip #1: Figure Out Your Blog Idea

The idea is where your publishing journey begins. Though you might not realize it, when you create your blog, you are creating a place where your future readers will come to get to know you and to care about what you have to say.

But what should your idea be?

There are a few ways to approach the idea that you have for your blog:

- Look at your competition to see what they're saying.
- Choose a topic that is related to your book.
- Write about something that you care deeply about, as readers will connect with that passion.

And here's a secret you will also want to keep in mind – you can adjust your idea and refine your idea as you create your blog.

What you will want to do is to choose an idea that is simple enough that people can relate, but one that is also expansive enough that you will have plenty to say about it.

Create a list of five possible blog ideas and then work your way through this section, as you'll find that one stands out about the rest in terms of uniqueness and in terms of effectiveness.

Tip #2: Choose a Memorable Name or Catch Phrase

Once you have an idea (or several ideas), start brainstorming about the possible titles you might have for your blog or a catchphrase for your blog.

For example, if you're talking about writing, then you might want to use something that makes readers interested to learn more. If you look at writing blogs, you will find that they often include titles about ideas, about creativity, etc.

Find something that will become memorable about your blog idea and then craft it into a memorable name. This will allow your readers to instantly remember who you are and what you have to offer.

Keep things short and sweet so that it's easy enough to recall – and to use as an actual website address.

Tip #3: Start a Blog (or Restart Your Blog)

If you haven't already started your blog, then it's time to begin. And if you have a blog set up already, then it's time to start thinking about how you can rebuild it.

You have a number of options when it comes to creating a blog. The most utilized blog publishers are:

- Wordpress – www.wordpress.com
- Blogger – www.blogger.com

These are both free blogging services that allow you to choose from a number of templates that will help you not only have a blog in place, but also create an attractive blog.

You will need to choose a name for the blog (which you should have ready at this point) and then choose the design. While you might change the design in the future as you learn more about blog design, right now the goal is to get started.

Tip #4: Get Writing

What you write in your blog is what will attract readers to your place in the Internet. You need to start writing about topics that interest you and that you think will interest your readers.

Some ideas for blog entries include:

- A personal introduction – Tell others who you are and why you're blogging in the first place.

- Market-relevant blogs – Discuss ideas related to the market you want to target, and give your thoughts and opinions.

- Anything – What's key in the beginning is simply creating blog entries that are available for others to read. At first, you want to fill up your blog with interesting blogs that appeal to your target market.

Your blog becomes the place where people come to see what you might say next. Though you have the bigger goal of having your book published, remember that these blogs are also a way to connect with your audience.

To connect with your audience, you need to speak honestly and clearly about what you care about, including your book.

Try to establish a regular routine on your blog, i.e. so many blog entries per week, on certain days of the week. With this schedule, your readers will know when to come back to learn more.

(And ask your readers to comment on what you've said. This will show you what your readers really want to hear about… and these comments can give you even more fuel for your writing.)

HOW TO BLOG EFFECTIVELY

Blogging is so simple, and yet many aren't quite sure how to make it work for their publishing goals. While you might understand how to write a book, the blog format can be challenging, as it seems as though you're speaking out into oblivion.

Tip #5: Interact with Your Audience

The key to impactful and effective blogging is to make sure you're not just speaking AT your readers. Instead, engage them and make them interested in responding.

This might happen in the form of a question at the end of your blogs or perhaps a controversial subject. When you make a reader want to continue the conversation, this will boost your market visibility and it will show the readers that you are a 'real' person.

Ask for comments and ask for ideas about future blogs. In doing so, you will begin to create more action on your blog, which leads to publishing sales later.

And don't just read the comments and nod your head when you see them pop up. Answer your commenters and thank them for their comments. If there's something particularly interested in one of the comments, you can use it for your next blog entry.

Plus, when you do this, you will show your readers that they might have a blog entry devoted to them…which also encourages more interaction.

Tip #6: Encourage Sharing

Your mother always told you to share, and your blog is the perfect place for you to encourage this behavior as well.

Once you have posted a blog, make sure you include buttons or some sort of sentence that encourages your readers to share your blog post on Twitter, on Facebook, etc. The more that the blog entry gets around, the more readers you can pull in.

While you obviously can't 'make' your readers share what they have read, the more interesting you are, and the more you praise the sharing of your posts, the more your words will get around.

Tip #7: Be Yourself

Finding your voice in your blog can be one of the more challenging parts of being a blogger. While you might know what you want to talk about, it can be difficult (at first) to understand what your voice is.

The best advice is to be yourself. It can help to speak aloud into a voice recorder to see what you sound like and then try to incorporate this way of speaking into your blogs.

Yes, it's not always grammatically perfect, but it's authentic. Over time, you will begin to develop an even more refined writing style. For now, however, the best thing to do is to be yourself and to be honest about who you are.

People connect with honesty, plus when you're honest, you don't need to think about how to sound. You're just being you.

USING YOUR BLOG AS A STARTING POINT FOR PUBLISHING

The blog might be a free tool at your disposal, but it's also a starting point for your publishing goals. In this space, you create a fan base in which you can begin to promote your ideas and your brand.

While you might not think you need to think about this just yet, the more that you can develop your blog now, the more results you will see in a shorter amount of time.

Tip #8: Build Your Brand

The success of your book begins with a brand. And by that, this means that you need to decide what you have to offer that others do not. This becomes the identity that you share and the way that you approach every single blog entry.

For example, if you consider yourself to be a nutritional guru, then you need to make sure that you take that sort of idea and build it into a brand. You can do this in a number of ways:

- Have a congruent blog name and catch phrase

- Have a certain way that sign off of each blog
- Create a bio that includes your brand idea and identity

The key is that once you have considered what your brand is and what you have to offer, you will continuously bring this idea up so that anyone who thinks of 'nutritional guru' will think of your name or your blog name.

Branding is something that large companies use frequently in their marketing strategies because the more repetition an idea gets; the more it sticks with the audience.

Tip #9: Mention Your Grand Book Idea

Once you've established your blog and you've begun to develop your brand, then it's time to start talking about your book idea.

Now, you might already have the book written or you just might be thinking about writing a book – it doesn't matter where you are. What does matter is that you begin to bring out the book that you have to share.

You might begin to create a blog entry around what your book will offer and what it has to teach. Or you might begin to discuss your book as a sort of side note in your blog entries, with the idea that you will pique the interest of an already captivated audience.

This is not necessarily about selling your book, but more about sharing the idea that you have created a book, something you think your audience will value, and that you wanted to make sure that you mentioned it.

Once you mention it, then you can continue to mention it every now and then if it's already been released.

Or if you're still in the releasing stage, then you may want to slowly increase how much you talk about your book until it is available to the public, building up the suspense.

Tip #10: Offer Free Sections of Your Book Through Your Blog

One way to add to your blog and to continue to create interest in the book you have to sell is to offer free sections of your book through your blog.

You might use a section of your book as a blog entry, and then ask for comments and feedback. This isn't necessarily about finding out if your audience is interested, but more about helping them see what you're all about with your writing.

Plus, everyone likes to get something for free.

Tip #11: Share Your Book News ONLY on Your Blog

Another key tip with a blog is to make your audience feel as though they're special for being on your blog...because they are.

You have, effectively, chosen the audience of your blog by writing to their interests and creating a dialogue you feel they would understand. You should thank them for their support by only announcing the book news on your blog.

And make sure that your audience knows this.

When the audience realizes they are privy to information others are not, they may then want to share this with others, extending the reach of your blog and of your book.

Be clear about the fact that you will ONLY post updates about the book on your blog, so everyone should stay tuned...and they should tell their friends to stop by your blog as well if they're interested.

THE PERSONAL BLOGGING EXPERIENCE (NOW WITH VIDEO!)

But you might be thinking that blogging has become so common that you may not stand out in the crowds of authors. And to a certain extent, this is true.

This isn't to say that you should step away from blogging — far from it. What you can do is make blogging even more personal and even more interactive with simple technology you probably already have in your office — video.

Tip #12: Add Video Blogs

Instead of just focusing on writing your blog entries, why not sit down with your webcam or your digital camera and talk about what you're interested in?

You can then post these video blogs on your blog site and be able to show your audience who you are and what you're really like. This connects in a way that allows your readers to feel as though they're in your home and that you're speaking to them as a friend, rather than as an authority.

While you do want to present yourself as an authority, or at least a highly informed person, on your subject matter, bringing your face and your voice into the blog will make you even more memorable.

You don't have to use video for every blog post, but it can certainly help to create something more interesting than just words on a page.

(And you can even include a transcript of the words you share in the blog, for those who want to read what you've said at a later time or for those with slower Internet connections.)

Tip #13: Address Reader Questions

Engaging your audience is the key to blogging success. No matter what you do and no matter what your goals are, you need to make your audience feel like they are people you genuinely care about.

One way to show that you care about your audience is to ask them what questions they have about you, your blog, your book, etc.

Once a week or once a month, ask for reader questions and then set up a certain day of the week when you will address these questions in a video blog. You will be able to talk directly to that reader and show them that you want to address them directly.

Or you can write out a blog piece and quote the reader's question. In either case, the readers of your blog then know you are listening and they know you're not just talking to yourself in hopes of promoting something.

Tip #14: Talk about Your Personal Life (to Connect!)

The Internet can be a fairly anonymous place, a place where you might not want to share too much about yourself since you're not sure who will read it or see it.

But that's no way to treat your blogging audience.

You need to become a real person and that means you need to share more about your life and who you are. There's no need to give out your home address, but you will want to talk about things you like and things you don't like.

Show off your personality and try a little humor (if that's who you are) when you're blogging. The more you do this, the more you will begin to relate to your audience, not just speak with them.

Some bloggers will have certain things they always talk about in their blogs, i.e. how they're drinking too much coffee. You want to bring in small personal details as this not only makes you more authentic, but it also encourages your readers to share their lives too.

Tip #15: Don't Make It All About Your Book

Because you do have the greater goal of publishing your book, it can be tempting to focus only on your book when writing your blogs. But this can actually work in the opposite way you want it to.

When you ONLY talk about your book, you're going to put some readers off. They can begin to interpret this as being more of a sales pitch than a blog, which is not necessarily a positive branding decision.

Instead, talk about your book occasionally, but talk more about the issues that surround your book. When you do this, then you will gently push readers into the decision of buying your book, but they don't feel as though you're trying to sell them on your ideas.

Focus on building up who you are and on that connection. While you might begin to think this has been stated too often, the idea of connecting with your audience is something you cannot forget.

3 BOOKS

Creating a book is a bit like giving birth, some authors would tell you. They had an idea that grew and grew until it was suddenly a fully formed novel or manuscript.

It wasn't always planned and it wasn't always clear what direction the idea might take, but eventually, it began to form in their mind. While this might not be what you're feeling right now, the creation of a book is certainly a way to become published, either by standard publishers or via self-publishing.

But where do you begin?

TO BOOK OR NOT TO BOOK?

Writing a book does not happen in an instant, or even in a week. Creating a book does happen after you've carefully selected an idea and decided how it can appeal to your audience.

With that in mind, it's true you could come up with any idea, write a book on it, and then put it before an audience. But this is also not the best plan. While you might have a book at the end, remember that you also want to have an audience when you're done.

And if your finished book doesn't engage them or impress them, you may not have another shot to get it right.

Tip #16: Find a Unique Idea...

Every great book began with a great idea. Though you might not have this idea just yet, you probably have some semblance of an idea in your mind. After all, if you had no idea about your book, you probably wouldn't be spending time thinking about how to publish it.

The key is to find out what ideas you have and what makes them uniquely yours.

As you've been building a blog and building a brand for yourself, it's time to consider what you bring to the proverbial table. What idea is uniquely yours and what idea is uniquely able to create an impression or solve a problem your audience has?

Right now, start thinking about the idea that you have and put it in the middle of a piece of paper. From that point, start drawing lines out from that idea to see what comes up for you, meaning what other ideas you have that stem from that main idea.

As you complete this exercise, think about what unique ways you can approach your idea. For example, if you're still talking about nutrition, then you might want to write a book about the ways that you can have high-end food with a small town budget.

The goal is not only to find an idea, but also to find an idea that's uniquely yours.

Use booksellers to look up other books on similar topics and then see how you can make them even more unique.

Tip #17: Take a New Look at an Old Idea

It's really the oldest form of art – taking an old idea and turning it into something new. (Or at least making something SOUND as though it's new.)

Start thinking about the topics you might want a book of yours to cover. Look at old topics that are popular with your blog audience and see how you can put your own personal spin on them. This might be a new outlook, a new attitude, or updated terms.

Ever wonder why there are so many successful weight loss books out there? Even though they're all covering the same material, they're doing well because they are using new pathways to the same goal – and it's a popular goal.

Tip #18: Use What You Teach and Know Well

Of course, the easiest way to write a book is to write about something you know and something that you know well.

Think about what you know well and what you could teach with others, so that you can create a book that shows you to be the expert on the topic.

While you might not have a degree in the subject matter, if you have the experience and you're able to teach what you know, you will connect with your audience in an effective way.

Plus, since you already know the topic, you won't have to do as much research, which is going to save you time.

Tip #19: Niche Research

One of the most effective ways to choose a topic for your book is to start doing some niche research. This means you're going to look into the specific market and see what people want to read.

You can do this in a number of ways:

- Looking at keyword trends online
- Looking at book sales in your market
- Reviewing other blogs and websites
- Asking your blog readers

When you're doing this research, take notes on what you find and what sounds unique to you. While you might see that a number of people are still interested in weight loss, that doesn't mean you need to make that the focus of your book.

Instead, you might want to your nutritional guru expertise, while giving some pages over to weight loss. In that way, you still address the market needs, while also focusing on what makes you excited.

TYPES OF BOOKS TO CREATE

You want to publish a book or you want to write a book, but there's more to the story (no pun intended) than that.

There are different kinds of books you can create, all with their own positive qualities, as well as additional ways to create income for you, as well as brand awareness and identity.

After all, you don't just want to have one book upon which to base your future, do you?

Tip #20: Think about Series

It's true – your audience doesn't want to only hear from you once when you're writing a book. Since the typical book can be read within a few weeks, even for the slower readers, you can't simply stop with one book.

First of all, that's not an income stream, and second, it's not going to serve your audience.

Your audience is constantly asking, 'What's next?' when they finish a book. And if you entertained or informed them with the first book, they're nearly guaranteed to want to find out what else you have to say.

Think about writing a series of books about your subject matter. Just as the Dummies books have been so popular and effective, you too can create a series of books that allow you to continue to pull in your audience and that continue to enhance your writing reputation.

But the most important thing to bear in mind as you're creating your series is to maintain consistency throughout. The Dummies series has succeeded because readers have come to know ahead of time what the reading experience is going to be. This means you have to make sure you have a strong design template so the look, feel, and approach of the books are identical across the series. This is often easier said than done.

Tip #21: Complementary Book Ideas

But there might be a book in you that's not necessarily something that can develop into a series. If you're writing about something that only has one main angle, then you may only have one book about that particular and narrow topic.

However, what else can you give to your reader?

What you might not realize right now is that when you create a book, there's always an opportunity for complementary books as well. These might include nutritional books if your main book is a weight loss book, or books about creating a bird watching vacation plan if your main book is about bird watching.

The key is to think about the other questions your readers might have once they are done reading your first book.

How can you enhance their knowledge?

How can you expand their experience?

Consider how you might create smaller complementary books that ensure your readers hear from you more often, and that they feel they can turn to you for a wider perspective.

Tip #22: Don't Limit Yourself to Books

And while it might be comforting to stick with just books when you're publishing, this is not the only way to engage an audience.

Plus, with the growing emphasis on e-readers and on digital media, readers aren't just looking for paperbacks or hardbacks anymore. They want to have more options at their fingertips – literally.

You might begin with the traditional book setup, but this is certainly not where you should stop your publishing endeavors.

MAKING MONEY WITH EBOOKS

eBooks are continuing to expand in terms of publishing presence. While more people turn to the iPad and the Kindle as virtual bookshelves, writers can't ignore the idea of digital writing and publication.

Since eBooks are cheaper to create and cheaper to disperse (often instantly), this format is a great way to keep your audience inside your inner circle.

Tip #23: Give Something Away

But there are still some readers who think eBooks are somehow 'less' of a book than a traditional book format is. And that makes sense, honestly. Since there isn't anything to hold, a reader might believe the eBook is going to be of a lesser quality.

You can't perpetuate this stereotype.

Instead, create eBooks that you can disperse on your website or your blog, but make sure they're just as high quality as anything else you'd write.

When you do this, you show your reader that quality can be had, even in an electronic format, plus you continue to build trust. This trust will allow you to increase your chances of selling more books when the time comes for you to do so.

Give something away. It doesn't have to be long, but it does have to offer something valuable to your reader. And once they read it, they can't wait to see what else you have to offer…even if they have to pay for it.

Tip #24: Sell a Part/Sample Chapter

Once you have your readers hooked with a free eBook, then it's time to start selling your 'real' book. You can even spread this out over time by selling parts of your book or sample chapters via Amazon.

In doing so, the reader doesn't have to commit to buying a whole book, and the lower price allows them to be more likely to make the decision to hand over their credit card information.

When this happens, they become more accustomed to buying from you, which will lead them to buying more from you in the future.

While many readers will want to just buy an entire book, having sample chapters and small portions for sale is just what some people in your audience need to ensure they're making the right choice.

Tip #25: Think about Different Supplementary Products

But it's not just about reading when it comes to selling your ideas in the book form.

True, many readers prefer the book format, but think about other things you can sell that are complementary:

- Audio CDs
- Workbooks
- Spiral bound journals
- Calendars
- Worksheets
- Supplies

You get the idea. Think about other ways that you can support your reader in the ways that the book educates them. You wouldn't just sell a reader an exercise video and then not give them the opportunity to buy the proper equipment from you too, would you?

Of course not.

Think about what might go well with your book (ideally things that you might use in the book or instruct the reader on using) and then offer those in addition to the book itself.

The more you can give to your audience, the more they are likely to purchase at the same time.

SOCIAL MEDIA
4

The social aspect of publishing is another way to increase your chances of success and another way to engage with your audience. Remember, when the audience is engaged, they are more likely to purchase your book and create a buzz around your ideas.

Thankfully, social media has made it easy to interact, if you know how to utilize these vast resources.

FACEBOOK

While you might already have a Facebook page for your personal use, you will also want to look into Facebook as a tool for publishing success.

Tip #26: Get an Author/Business Page

You can begin by creating a separate page for either your book or for yourself if you plan on creating a series of books. You simply need to create a new page or group that will allow you to interact with your audience.

Go to a page or a group to which you already belong and you'll find on the left side a link to create your own page or group. Fill in the details and you're ready to start inviting people to your group, where you can then engage with them regularly.

Tip #27: Be Active

It's simply not enough to create a page and expect everyone to interact on their own. You need to be instrumental in the activity that occurs on the page.

Whether you add links to your blog postings or you update your status each day, you will want to make sure you're on the page just as much as your audience may be.

A great way to approach this is to make sure you're signing into the page and updating it during the time zones when most of your audience will also be active.

Tip #28: Answer Your Messages

When you receive messages or comments on your Facebook page, you will want to reply to them as quickly as possible during your working hours.

(And in the beginning of your page, you might want to respond even more quickly and more frequently.)

In doing so, you will ensure that you are showing up as a reliable person and that you are creating the ideal rapport with your audience.

Tip #29: Advertise

You can also utilize the Facebook advertising system in order to reach even more audience members. All you need to do is to sign up for Facebook's advertising program (which is a paid service) and then advertisements for your book(s) will show up on pages where your likely audience members will be.

When they search for a certain keyword or they show that they are active in the same markets, they will see your advertisement and be led to your website or your blog for more information – or to make a purchase.

TWITTER

Twitter is another tool that is like a blog, only much, much shorter. While it's often become a place where people post any old details about their lives, you can also use this service to lead your book to publishing success.

In just 140 characters.

Tip #30: Check in Frequently

Just as with any social media tool, your best chance of success comes from becoming and staying active on Twitter. You should continue to post new tweets throughout the day, helping to show that you are someone with things to share and ideas of value.

These tweets can be simple sentences about your work, bits from your blog, links to your blog posts, etc.

The key is to post things that are of value to your target market so that you're coming up as an expert in your field, and others will begin to take notice of what you have to say.

Tip #31: Get the Right Followers

Of course, just posting anything on Twitter is not enough to lead yourself to publishing success. Instead, you need to make sure that you're posting things of value to the right followers.

But how can you get the 'right' followers?

At first, you will want to follow people who seem to have an interest in what you have to say. You can search for these accounts via the Twitter search function.

Start following those people and then start talking to them. Once you do, you will begin to amass even more followers, without having to seek them out on your own.

Tip #32: Interact with Others

Indeed, the key with making Twitter an effective social media tool is to interact with others when they interact with you, or to engage with others when you have something to share.

For example, if someone on your Twitter feed has a question related to your book's topic, you might want to answer his or her query. This shows you are interested in helping others, while also showing your knowledge.

You don't simply want to reply to others with your book link, though you will want to include that once you have established a strong Twitter following.

Tip #33: Retweet, Retweet

When you're on Twitter, you might notice there are links related to what you have to share in your book. In these cases, make sure that you retweet these links and posts so that you're showing your support of these Twitter members.

In doing so, you will create the shared experience of social media, allowing you the chance to be engaged. And when you share others' links, they are more likely to share yours as well.

Just by retweeting other links, your Twitter handle (name) will show up in the feeds more often, helping to spread the word about your existence and to encourage more followers.

Tip #34: Don't Just Schedule Your Tweets

Yes, it's true there are a number of handy services (which we'll talk about later) that can schedule your tweets in advance. While this is certainly convenient for you, the trick is that it's not true engagement.

As you post links ahead of time or you set up tweets to run when you're not around, you might begin to show that you're someone who doesn't actually care about engagement.

It's not a bad thing to schedule your tweets in advance, but make sure that you're not relying on this service for all of your tweets.

You want to be present in the discussions as well, talking with other Twitter followers and showing that you're listening even more than you're sharing your own thoughts.

LINKEDIN

For many people, LinkedIn has become the place for professional social media sharing. This is a fine tuned social media site where professionals can post their credentials and their job histories, helping to showcase their expertise within a given field.

Even if you don't feel like you're an expert in your book's chosen market (not yet, anyway), you will want to post facts about your background on LinkedIn, as it's a place that holds more weight in terms of reliability.

Tip #35: Set up Your Profile

To begin, you need to set up your LinkedIn profile. This includes your business name, your name, your website address, etc.

Fill out all of the areas that you can, and include the training and related work you've done in your chosen market.

When you do this, you will begin to see others who might be connected to your line of work, and that's where the social media experience can truly begin.

Tip #36: Get Involved in Groups

LinkedIn also has groups, much like the groups on Facebook, that will allow you to be a part of discussions related to your book's market and topic.

By engaging in these conversations, you can begin to meet others and you can see what the market is currently discussing, helping you to refine your ideas.

In addition, these groups can help you establish another following outside of your other audiences.

Tip #37: Connect!

When you're in the LinkedIn system, you will connect with others to begin to share your information more easily. You can connect with people you know or you can reach out to those who you feel offer similar services.

As you do this, you will begin to show off your profile to a wider audience, who can then connect to you, get to know you, and begin to understand what you have to offer.

While there is some debate (as in all social media contexts) about whether you should connect with people you don't actually know in real life, since you may never meet your customers in the real world, this is a great starting point for connecting to new faces.

Tip #38: Start a Group

Yes, you could join a number of groups that allow you to interact with others, or you can start your own LinkedIn group to begin the discussion yourself.

Others can then join these groups, and as you continue to discuss in this system, you will begin to increase your visibility, which will allow you the opportunity to have more connections and more perceived value.

Tip #39: Update Often

While this may begin to be a mantra for you when you're working on the success of your publishing future, just as with anything, you need to update your LinkedIn profile and status often.

You need to reevaluate your profile and your activity each week, allowing you the chance to show that you're ever evolving in your niche.

And the more involved you are, the more exciting you become to others.

Tip #40: Look for New Contacts Often

As you set up your LinkedIn profile, you can reach out to others with your email address book. This is a great starting point, but also set aside time each week to search for people (often in the groups you join) that might make good connections.

Ask others to become a part of your LinkedIn community and you will continue to grow your following.

OTHER SOCIAL MEDIA OPTIONS

Social media is ever expanding and there are always new options you can explore in terms of creating awareness of your book and your ideas.

That said, it could also seem a little overwhelming when you're first starting out.

Instead of trying every possible social media outlet, it's often a better idea to find a few that you find simple (i.e. Facebook and Twitter), and then when you have a following there, then move onto new options, like the ones listed next.

Tip #41: Google+

Like Facebook, Google+ is a place where you can set up a profile and share information with others who are in your circles. This service is unique as it allows you to create different levels of engagement, depending on what you want to do.

If you want to share certain pieces of information with friends, you can by placing them in your friends circles. Or you can create other circles that allow you to target your ideas to the audiences you feel will benefit the most.

Tip #42: Tumblr

Tumblr is another place where you can begin to reach out to your chosen audience. This is another blogging format where you can post your ideas and your thoughts, allowing you to continue to stay engaged with your audience or your intended audience.

Tip #43: Hub Pages

Since customers want to know that you're an expert in your field, thus increasing their ability to trust you, you can also sign up for Hub Pages. This is a service where you can create a hub that's devoted entirely to your chosen market.

In this hub, you will post articles that are relevant and people can share them, comment on them, and like them. The more popular your hub, the more popular you can become in the overall market and online.

This is a bit more than a blog as you want to create information-filled posts that offer value, so those who are experts in their fields may want to utilize this service.

Tip #44: Pinterest

When you're the creative type, a newer social media site called Pinterest is a place where you can share your ideas and your visions. You can post pictures on this site and you can begin to establish a less wordy version of your life and your work.

This is often a welcome relief to those audience members who don't have time to spend on reading new blog entries.

Instead, they can look at your boards of pictures and share their own ideas too.

(Hint: You might want to post possible book designs here.)

Tip #45: Twaitter

Now, yes, we've already talked about how you probably shouldn't schedule all of your Twitter posts. But there are going to be times when you just don't have the energy or you're not around to post on Twitter.

With Twaitter (a.k.a. Gremlin for some), you can schedule your tweets long into the future, ensuring that your Twitter feed never goes bare, even when you're sleeping or you're on vacation.

Tip #46: Hootsuite

Hootsuite acts in a similar way to Twaitter/Gremlin, but it can also include options for scheduling posts for Facebook pages and accounts. You can also schedule your tweets here, so this becomes a place where you can handle all of your social media at once, on one single page.

Tip #47: Tweetdeck

Tweetdeck is another tool that you can install onto your computer to help you connect with others, via the scheduling of tweets. That said, this tool also helps you to see the posts of others so you can more easily reply to what other followers have shared.

Tip #48: Posterous

Once more, creative types that want to be more visual in their posts can use Posterous to help them create a picture connection with their market audience. In doing so, you can quickly post from your iPhone or Android, helping to always have a way to connect with your audience, even when you're on the road.

Plus you can include text so you have the best of both worlds with this option.

Tip #49: Ning

When you're ready to dive into more intensive discussions with your audience members, you can create a Ning group that allows you to establish a small and private community.

Many writers will use Ning for special members, even creating paying memberships. This will allow you to post even more exclusive content here, provided that people sign up and pay.

Ning is also a community where the members can interact with each other. This shared experience can help to boost your overall reputation in your market.

SOCIAL MEDIA ADVICE

You're beginning to think that social media is going to take up your writing time, aren't you? While this is certainly a common concern for those who are interested in using social media often to lead them to publishing success, there are strategies you can employ to use it effectively.

And efficiently.

Tip #50: How Often

While there are no hard and fast rules as to how often you should post with social media, a good rule of thumb is to make sure you're posting at least once a day, at a regular time.

When you do this, your audience will know to expect your post and they will either look for them later or meet up with you then.

Others will say that you should post as often as possible, which does sound like a good way to engage, but it's not sustainable and many audience members might begin to feel overwhelmed by all of the posts they 'have' to read.

Tip #51: What to Say

In social media, you can say anything you like, but here's what you should keep in mind with each post you create:

- Does this add value?
- Have I thought about the impact of this post?
- Will I inspire community engagement?

Think about your audience in every post you make, and that will guide you to the right things to say, no matter how often you decide to post.

Tip #52: Cross Posting

Another concern in the social media debate is the idea of cross posting.

The issue is this: should you post the same posts across your Twitter, Facebook, and other accounts?

Yes and no. The truth is that your audience will probably sign up for all of your social media options, and they don't necessarily want to have all of the same ideas coming at them ten times a day.

But, that doesn't mean you need to be completely unique either. You might want to have related posts on the sites; helping to decrease the time you spend creating these posts.

Or you might want to post at different days on these sites to ensure you're not posting the same links every day, but that you're still keeping up with sharing the ideas you have.

Tip #53: To Schedule or Not to Schedule?

Scheduling your social media is going to be necessary after a while. The key with doing this well is to make sure you're not relying on it too heavily, unless you're posting things that aren't going to be live on your website or your blog ahead of time.

You might want to schedule some things like:

- Motivational quotes
- Relevant sales pitches – i.e. upcoming releases, sales, etc.

But you also need to intersperse these posts with live posts from you.

That said, you might be able to create posts that sound as though you're actually available on the Internet at that time.

For example, if a holiday is coming up, you might schedule a post to be related to that holiday.

The key is to make sure you're responding to the responses you get so that it's clear that you're not just posting to post.

Tip #54: How to Keep Up with Posts

Managing a large Facebook group or Twitter following can certainly present its challenges. You want to respond to everyone, but it's not possible – no matter how much caffeine you might drink.

Instead, you need to focus more on the VALUE that your social media interactions will provide.

You need to start by responding to as many posts as possible, as many direct messages as possible, etc.

But after a time, you may want to be clear about when you will actually be on line checking in with your social media. In doing so, you will keep your time online to a minimum, and you will draw in those who want to hear directly from you.

And make sure you stick to your promised times.

Tip #55: Time to Get Help?

When you have generated a lot of followers, it might very well become time to hire someone else to help you.

This might be a social media manager who understands what you want to present in your posts and can follow the way that you write or speak. While many of the bigger social media names are certainly doing their own posts, they also have help because they need to keep up…and they still need to sleep at night.

MORE ADVICE
5

The advice that will help lead you to publishing success is more than one book can contain. But when it comes to helping you right now, there is more you can learn, outside of marketing and outside of advertising.

You need to know how to create published works that have value for your audience – and sometimes, you need to step beyond the book format as you know it.

GUIDEBOOKS

Many of your audience members will not only want to learn from you, but they'll want to be guided by you to a certain solution or state of mind.

With guidebooks, you can create a clear definition of who you are, what you have to offer, and how others can do it too. If you've spent any time looking around the Internet at others in the blogging world and publishing market, you'll see hundreds of guidebooks that outline the specifics for hungry readers.

Tip #56: How to Guide

The guidebook is a way to bring people into your internal thought process and into the inner workings of who you are and what you do.

For example, if you run a successful writing business, you might write a book that outlines step by step how you did it. In doing so, you clearly help the reader accomplish the same goal, and they have the faith in your instructions as you've already shown that you have been a success.

Tip #57: What to Guide

Readers are hungry to learn more about 'how to' do something. They don't just want to learn about something, they want to know EXACTLY how to do it.

Too many times, books are written without a clear definition of what the reader should so with the knowledge, but you don't have to continue this trend.

Think about:

- How to do _____ well.
- How to create _____ in _____ steps/days/years

Consider the topic that your book covers and then create a guide that helps the reader move through a process. Think of this as a sort of course that will allow the reader the opportunity to truly grasp the content you have to share.

When the content becomes action, the reader feels valued and they begin to share with others that you are not only an expert, but also a guide.

Tip #58: How to Create Guidebooks

Creating guidebooks is simple once you have the idea in your mind. What you want to do is to think about something that you can guide a person to do.

From there, break the steps up on a piece of paper or on your computer and then decide what a reasonable amount of time might be for each section to be learned.

Some people like to create guidebooks based on steps in a project, while you might find that a calendar is more effective. No matter what you choose, make sure that you break things up into smaller pieces.

Tip #59: Pictures and Videos

To ensure your reader is clear about the words you share in your guidebook, it can help to include pictures and videos. These will help those readers who learn visually.

Combined with words in a book, you cannot only reach out to different learners, but you can ensure that your words are effective and clear.

You might also want to consider having more extensive video packages, but more on that in a minute.

Tip #60: When to Guide

The trickiest part of guiding your audience is knowing WHEN you want to guide them.

If you've put our your book and it's been successful, you may begin to get feedback from your readers that they want more. They want to know exactly how to create the results that you've expressed in words.

But the truth is that even if you don't get this sort of feedback, you will want to provide a follow up guidebook as close to the publication date of your initial book as possible.

When you do this, you are giving the reader every chance to make sure they're able to generate the success you want to see for them.

VIDEO TRAINING

While we've already alluded to it, not everyone is a book learner. Though it's true that you want to get into book publishing, people want more than that, and some might NEED more than that.

With videos and video training, you can connect on another level, making sure your audience is truly given all of the possible tools to make their lives better...while also making sure your publishing efforts lead to success.

Tip #61: Brainstorm Videos

From the beginning of writing your book, you may have already begun to think of videos that might complement your work. You have thought about how you could express your ideas in video format, allowing you the chance to ensure your audience truly 'gets' what you're trying to say.

Right now, take some time to think about all of the potential videos you can create that are related to your book.

Even if the videos aren't directly complementary to your book, they can provide an additional layer of information.

Tip #62: The Equipment You Need

One obstacle that people feel stands in the way of their ability to make videos that relate to their books is equipment.

Many people think they need to have expensive equipment in order to make a decent video to sell. This is not the case.

While it's true that the more successful you get, the more you will want to invest in your technology, right now, that's not necessary. You simply need a decent digital video recorder (even your webcam), a basic light set up, and a computer that can edit videos.

Most computers now come with video editing software, so this is not generally a new expense for anyone.

Take some time to learn about each of the tools you have and then make a few test videos of yourself talking. You will be surprised at how clear the pictures are once you practice a bit and try out different lighting arrangements.

Tip #63: Training Formats/Products

The videos that you create should offer something that a person can use while they're watching the video.

Think about the success of exercise videos, for example. These videos simply create a workout that a person follows while they are watching. You can create the same training video, even if you're not talking about exercise.

Some ideas include:
- Step by step instructions
- Seminar formats
- Interviews with experts
- Screen capture videos for technology training

You can create nearly anything on a training video so long as it shows what a person needs to do, when they need to do it, and how they need to do it in order to be a success.

It can help for you to review other training videos in your market to see what your competition is already offering and then make sure you create something similar (with different content, of course).

Tip #64: Length of Training

But how long should a training video be? It shouldn't be so long that a person will not watch all of the video and it should not be so short that it seems like the person on the other end isn't getting any value for their time.

Keep in mind that the human brain only focuses well for about 90 minutes. Anything long than this is going to create learning issues for some.

A good tip is to keep the training videos to no more than one hour, and if you're targeting an audience that might be crunched for time, think about something shorter.

As always, think of your audience and what they expect from you so that you're creating a video that is actually effective for their needs.

Tip #65: Training Packages

You might want to create training packages that go along with the book that you have written. This will help you create something that is not only useful, but that can also be marketed separately.

The training package might include:
- Introduction video
- 7 day course – 7 videos for 7 topics
- A wrap up video

You can play around with the number of videos in the package, of course, but it might be helpful to include a workbook or a written outline of what the videos cover.

By having multiple tools in the training package, as well as worksheets, supplies, etc., not only can you charge more, but you can also build up your audience and ready them for future books, training packages, and so on.

Tip #66: Create High Quality Videos

When you're focusing on a topic that will require you to have a high quality video, there are a few things you will want to have available:

- High quality digital camera – akin to the Flip camera
- Basic video editing software
- Studio lighting
- Microphone and digital audio recorder

Though you don't necessarily need these items right now, the more expensive your setup, the crisper your videos will be.

Or if you don't want to invest in the equipment now, or ever, you can also hire someone to record your videos for you, and then let them handle the quality you want to create.

THE TRUTH ABOUT BOOK DESIGN

While they say you can't judge a book by its cover, it is certainly not the case in publishing today.

Not only will your audience judge your book by its design, but they will also tell others about the quality of your design, especially when it's clear you haven't spend the necessary time or energy.

Your words are the most important part of your book, but if the appearance is less than stellar, you're not going to keep the attention of your audience for long.

Tip #67: Organize Your Book

You have the ideas organized, but you also need to organize the text of your book in order to ensure your publishing success.

You can do this in several ways:

- Section titles
- Subheadings
- Bullet points
- Side boxes

- Table of contents
- Index

As you can see in this book, the main headings are larger than others, helping a reader easily navigate from page to page. When you make it clear what each section is about, the reader feels they are being led competently.

You might also want to think about organizing in a similar way to other related books on the market. Though this isn't about copying what others are doing, when your audience expects a certain layout, it never hurts to ensure you're giving it to them.

Tip #68: Book Layouts

The way your words are presenting in your book matters. Period. You can't simply put your words on a series of pages and then expect your reader to understand how things are supposed to be read.

While the reader certainly expects to read from front to back, it can help to consider new ways of engaging them in the process.

For example, some books are being published in the digital format and thus may be laid out in a landscape design as opposed to the normal page design.

Or you might want to choose a smaller layout that's specifically designed to look good on a Kindle or another e-reader.

Think once more about your audience, where they're most likely to read the book, and how you can make this easy and enjoyable.

Tip #69: Design Software

To help you with the layout and design process, it can help to invest in design software that is specifically created for book publishing.

InDesign by Adobe is one option, but there are others that you can use if you're on a Mac computer, as opposed to a PC. If you're going to do the layout and design on your own, you want to invest in something that other professionals use.

You could try to do the work with a basic word processing program, but this will look like…you just used your word processing program.

Though some audience members may never notice the difference, those that do tend to be more outspoken.

Tip #70: Professional or On Your Own?

All of this design talk brings up a good point – should you do your own design or should you have a professional do the heavy lifting for you?

It depends on your goals and your budget.

A book designer can be expensive, very expensive. They need to spend hours working on the best possible layout and working closely with you to ensure your vision is seen in the final product.

Now, when you're trying to be successful in publishing, this is an investment that you should make.

Tip #71: Design Really Matters

The design of your book not only helps you to organize the thoughts you have to share with your readers, but it will also help you to show just how serious you are about your book.

When you show that you care about what your book looks like and what it means to you, your audience will respond in kind.

Design allows you to:

- Create clarity.
- Show that you're not just another writer that wants to make money (instead, you want to make an impression).
- Guide the reader.

The design that you create now can also become 'your' design for the rest of your books.

You might also choose a design that is akin to what your blog or your website looks like, helping to continue your branding message and mood.

Tip #72: Save Design for Last?

With all of this design talk and all of this concern about what your book looks like, it sounds like something that is best left to the end.

And yes, that's often true.

At the same time, you will want to make sure you're thinking about what the end design *might* be so that you're writing with this structure in mind. The more you can do this from the start, the more you can create a finished product more quickly.

Of course, if you've already written your book, you'll (of course) leave the design for the end. Or now.

HYBRID PUBLISHING

The publishing world has changed and it's not going to go back to the way it was any time soon. For many authors, this is a delightful idea and for others it's created more questions than answers.

Take hybrid publishing, for example. Many people haven't heard the term, even though they are already engaging in this new way of approaching the book publishing path.

Tip #73: Why Hybrid Works

You've already figured out that taking just one direction isn't necessarily the best way to approach, well, anything. In the downed economy, those who had all of their eggs in the proverbial basket were disappointed to find those same eggs were missing.

And the fact they had no other baskets was not a stable financial plan.

With hybrid publishing, you're not limited to just one form of publishing your book, and thus you're not limited to just one stream of revenue or one path to success.

Hybrid works because it approaches audiences where they are – everywhere.

Instead of just being a self-published author or a traditionally published author, you can have a little of both and enjoy the benefits that come from having your feet in both doors.

Tip #74: Get Editing Help

You don't have to do everything yourself when you're on the path to publishing success. In fact, you may not want to do everything on your own.

Instead, start getting help for your book today so you can publish it quickly and get it on the market and out of your hands (and head).

An editor is a great investment for any writer that's been working on their book for an extended period of time. Instead of looking over the same words and truly believing they're perfect, you can call in someone that has perspective.

A professional editor will be able to tell you what needs to be changed, how it needs to change, and where your latest typo is.

While it's true that content is kind, if you have a lot of editing errors in your book, your audience isn't going to be impressed.

Tip #75: Get Design Help

You already know this, but get design help. You don't have to learn a new piece of software or navigate this creative side of your book's publication.

Instead, you can focus your time on coming up with new ideas for training programs, guide books, etc.

A designer can create an appealing cover and layout, allowing your words to look as good as they sound.

Tip #76: Get Writing Help

While you might think every book author out there writes his or her own words, this is not always the case. If you have great ideas and you want to be an author, but you don't want to spend the time learning how to write well, you can call on a ghostwriter.

This is a person who steps in to write your book, without taking any of the credit.

They can be found via traditional freelance channels, helping you to get your book onto the page, even if you're not the right person to write the actual book.

Tip #77: Do You Need an Agent?

For those who are looking at long-term publishing success, it can help to have an agent who can look for the publishing opportunities available.

This professional is going to do the work you don't have time for, plus they can offer you insight into what the market needs and what the publishers really want to see. Agents are also extremely valuable when it comes to contract negotiations and helping you understand everything from publishing legalese to determining royalty structures. Most traditional publishers will not even consider working with an author who doesn't have an agent. There are a few but good luck finding them.

For most, the idea of an agent is something they may want to look into now, but they may not need an agent for some time to come.

But for the hybrid publishing world, you can look into this traditional support while still self-publishing your book until the agencies come looking for you.

Tip #78: Self Publishing Works

Let's be honest here — if you're only sending your book out to major publishing houses and your name isn't Janet Evanovich or J.K. Rowling, chances are good it might take a while to hear back.

In the meantime, you will want to try out self-publishing. It not only works, but it's also been a vehicle for a number of successful authors today.

(Including J.K. Rowling.)

Self publishing is the process in which you create your book and then you have someone else print it for you to sell through your online store or even out of the back of your car.

You have full control over how your book is used, what its price might be, and how you distribute it.

And you can sell your book through places like Amazon, which allows you to be your own publishing agency.

Tip #79: Be Your Own Agent

It's true. You can be your own literary agent as well, assuming that you want to learn more about writing contracts and the publishing industry.

However, as you self publish, and as you're waiting to hear back from a potential agent, you can act on your own behalf in legal situations, though I strongly recommend you get a publishing expert's opinion if you decide to go it alone. Publishing contracts are fairly standard across the board but language may vary as does the level of flexibility publishers have in terms of changing or striking certain clauses from the contract. You will want to know what those parameters are.

You can also talk directly to publishers to see how you might get your book published through traditional means. While you might not get responses immediately, the more that you begin to reach out to publishing agencies, the more you will learn about what they want to hear from you.

MORE PUBLISHING TIPS

The path to successful publishing can be very rewarding. At the same time, there is always more to learn, more to do, and more to say about your book in order to stir up publicity.

In this section, we're going to wrap up the 101 tips with marketing advice that will make sure you're selling your book – even if the big agencies never do.

(Of course, once they see how successful you are, they might just change their minds.)

Tip #80: Write Guest Blogs

When you see there are other blogs that are related to your book's blog, try asking the blog author if you can write a guest blog for them. This will help to expose you and your book to a new and related audience.

Tip #81: Teach Classes

If your book is based on something that you know well, see if you can arrange to teach a class on this topic in your local community or at a local school. Not only can you get paid and gain experience, but you can also market your books to the students.

Tip #82: Give Speeches

Many professionals in the blogging and publishing world today were able to crack through the industry's brick wall by going out and giving speeches through organizations like Toastmasters.

Not only will you begin to develop your public speaking skills, but you will also be able to stalk about the topics about which you are passionate, and that passion will be infectious to your audience.

Tip #83: Pricing Right

If you're self-publishing or handling other methods of publishing and sales, you need to know that the price is the final thing that will repel or attract a buyer to take action.

- You can't price too low – This will make the reader think your book doesn't offer value.
- You can't price too high – This might be out of the reader's price range.

This sounds a bit like the story of Goldilocks, doesn't it? Instead, you want to think about what other related books in your market are selling for.

Many eBooks and e-reader books will sell for less than a printed copy; so first consider the method of delivery and what it costs you. Next, look at your competition.

Then think about your audience and what they're willing to pay.

You can test the waters by offering your book at a lower rate for 24 hours. If a lot of people snatch up the book, then you might have priced too low, and if no one buys, then you might have priced too high.

In either case, you've learned something.

Tip #84: Marketing Materials

While most of your marketing and advertising seems to be online for publishing your book, don't limit yourself.

More traditional marketing materials can be very effective at trade shows, presentations, speeches, and in classes.

- Business cards
- Postcards with your book's cover as the main design

- Posters
- Magnets
- Pencils...

The key is to get your book's name and YOUR name out there. And investing in some of these tangible items can leave your readers with a lasting impression.

Tip #85: Translate Your Words

Another thought to make sure that your published book is a hit is to consider getting it translated into popular languages. In doing so, you will make your ideas relatable to others, while also expanding your market.

Since websites can be translated, you're already getting international readers, so why not offer them your book in their native tongue?

(Just look at your website statistics to find out where the most visitors are from and then figure out how to translate your book into the corresponding language.)

Tip #86: Don't Forget About Fiction

While much of the focus on book publishing is pointed at nonfiction, this doesn't mean you should completely discount the idea of fiction for your publishing success.

You can let your creativity loose with a story or with something that's a bit less serious. Even if you only sell it for a few dollars and you only write a few pages, you never know what else your audience wants until you write it and offer it to them.

Tip #87: Blog Relationships

The world of blogging is one in which everyone is committed to helping everyone else. When you develop strong blogging relationships, you can have others supporting you as you work to promote your book.

And this promotion can go both ways. You can promote the books of others, ones that don't conflict with your book, and the favor will be returned.

With this approach, you begin to create affiliates, of sorts, allowing your marketing message to be spread to a wider audience, without adding more effort on your part.

Tip #88: Do Some Good

Another great idea to add power to your publishing is to do good in your community. By contributing to charity events and by being active in the charitable causes related to your work, you can begin to change the way that your book is seen.

And you can boost the way you are seen by those in your audience now and in the future.

Try being a part of:

- Fundraisers
- Charitable games
- Health events

Or make sure that some of the profits of your book go toward a cause you believe in, and that is related to your book's content.

Tip #89: Team Up with Others

Whenever possible, you should try to team up with others to make your publishing endeavor more profitable. Instead of just going it alone, try to team up with others to sell your books together, especially when they're related topics.

You can see this model often online with the bigger names in blogging (i.e. Jonathan Mead). They will work with others in their market to sell items together as a part of a package, or they might work with you to add your book to their promotion package.

While you might not get paid for that book's sales, you will gain exposure, which often leads to more success in the future. Once your name is out there and connected to someone else who is a big name, you will be considered at his or her level of expertise.

Tip #90: Get a Website started

If you haven't already thought of it, you should begin your own website in addition to your blog. This can become a place where you are able to sell your book and to promote your brand.

You can easily start building your own website (or hire someone else to do the work for you) with the help of places like GoDaddy or Weebly.

Tip #91: Have a release party

If you have your book ready to go, do what the bigger publishers do – have a release party in your local community.

You can invite all of your friends and family, and get press coverage for the event from your local press.

When you do this, this continues to push your book into the market, allowing the biggest publishers to take notice of how successful you already are, even without their help.

Tip #92: Talk to Local Booksellers

Your local community already has the resources you need to start promoting your book and continuing to develop your audience.

Talk to local booksellers about selling your book and placing your book on their shelves. It's often easier to get your book on local bookstore shelves than it is to get your book in larger name stores.

You can also set up events at the local booksellers:

- Talks
- Book signings
- Parties

These will help to also introduce your face and then connect it with your book to create more streams of potential income.

Tip #93: The Right Bio

On your website and your blog, you should have a clear bio about who you are, what you have to offer, and what makes you unique. The reader wants to know who the face is behind the writing, so you need to develop a bio that is easy to read, easy to share, and compelling.

(And if you're unable to do this for yourself, hire a ghostwriter to handle this task.)

Tip #94: Your Press Packet

It can also help to be ready for the press that will inevitably want to cover your story once your publishing marketing strategies continue to get noticed.

This packet can include:

- Your bio
- A picture of yourself
- A picture of the book cover/postcard with details
- Press releases about your book

- Some blog entries
- Etc.

This packet is then something the press can use to learn more about you. And with this information, they can begin to develop a story that continues your publishing power.

Tip #95: Send Out Sample Copies

If you already have your book ready to go, it's time to start handing it out to people who might be interested. This way, you can get feedback and you can create a buzz even before you make it available to the public.

A tip: try to hand the book out to people who are already a part of your audience on your blog. This will not only make them feel special, but it will begin to create a conversation about what your book has to offer to those who you've written it for.

You can also send out sample copies to publishing houses and to other publishing agencies to see how they respond, and what they might be able to do for your publishing dreams.

Tip #96: Get Testimonials...NOW!

Those sample copies? You can hand them out, without expecting any feedback, or you can ask the readers for testimonials and reviews of the writing.

This will give you text to add to your website and blog, further stirring up the publishing message.

(Include the testimonials in your press packet too for more powerful proof of the book's appeal.)

Tip #97: Edit, Edit, Edit

While you have already edited your book at this point, since it's probably written and ready to go, it never hurts to have it edited again before you send it out to be sold.

Even the smallest typo can cause your book to lose its power and for you to lose your credibility.

Tip #98: Edit Again

And then edit the book again. No harm in being too careful with your hard work.

Tip #99: Thoughts about Ghostwriters

While you've already thought about ghostwriting for your work, you might want to remember that it's not just about the book that you've created right now.

If you want to keep up with the demand of your audience, it can help to start looking at ghostwriters to continue the flow of information. Once you already have a successful book, it's easier for a new writer to step in and create something similar. But in order for an author-ghostwriter partnership to work, you need to be comfortable with and trust one another, otherwise these relationships can be tough going.

Ghostwriters can also help with:

- Blog entries
- Social media
- Press releases
- Website content
- Splash pages
- Related articles on article directory sites

And more.

You need to keep producing after writing your book, as you haven't worked so hard to only have one book out there.

Tip #100: Planning Your Next Book

Speaking of your next book, though you may have spent all of your time and energy on the book before you, realize that you're only as successful as your NEXT book.

Publishers that might have heard of your success will be looking to see if you're going to be someone who can continue to be powerful with your audience next year, not just today.

Start thinking today about the book that you might write next, or you can turn to your audience to begin to create a set of new ideas.

- Ask in your blog entry
- Have contact information at the end of the book
- Only use half of your first book and use the second half for your next book

Focus on what ELSE you can provide so that your momentum keeps pushing you to publishing success.

Tip #101: Get Started Now!

And the most important tip of all: don't wait to write your book. Start today so that someone else doesn't get to your idea before you do.

You owe it to your idea to write now, market now, and spread the word today.

CONCLUSION
6

Your book publishing success is imminent, especially in today's market. While you might approach publishing differently and you might see that it's more about engaging an audience and cultivating trust before anything else, you can succeed.

And you now have 101 steps to take.

While trends change, people always want to know more. They want information that they can apply to their lives, that they can use to become better people, and that they can turn into action steps for their new plans in life.

Though it's true that books are fading from the bookstore shelves, this does not mean that books aren't powerful forces in the market today. The world has gone digital, and this means there's more opportunities for publishing success.

Anyone can do it, and now you can too.

Your path to publishing success begins right now.

But only you can lead the way.

APPENDIX

TOP TEN MISTAKES AUTHORS COMMONLY MAKE

This section is adapted from a feature that ran on www.networldingblog.com in January and February 2012 by Jon Malysiak, the co-founder and president of the Jonathan Scott Literary Agency in Chicago, Illinois.

Mistake #1: Assume That Your Work Is Done Once You've Turned in the Final Draft of the Manuscript

This is perhaps the most common misconception I've seen first-time authors make. Yeah, by all means revel in the sense of accomplishment you'll feel when you email that final draft off to your editor. It's a tremendous achievement and quite unlike anything you may ever have experienced. However... the truth is, while you may feel the worst is behind you, you're wrong. You may very well have written the next New York Times bestseller, but unless you are prepared to market the heck out of your book and yourself as an author, that precious accomplishment of yours is not going to sell. It just isn't. If no one knows who you are, no one's going to pick your book off the shelf or download it from Amazon.

So what does this mean? It means you need to be aggressively letting everyone you know—and more importantly, everyone you don't know—that you've published a book and that they need to go out and buy it. Sure, publishers have their in-house sales and marketing teams, but more often than not, they are going to rely on you to help them reach out to the marketplace. It's never too early to start the pitch process. I've seen all too many worthy projects fall by the wayside because the author hasn't been diligent in building his or her marketing platform. Quite simply, many publishers won't even consider acquiring a new project unless the author has a proven publicity track record. It's all about PLATFORM, PLATFORM, PLATFORM! This is perhaps the most overused word in the publishing lexicon. Get acquainted with it, make it your friend, and use it to your best advantage. Facebook, Linked-In, and Twitter are great places to start. If you don't an account with one of these social media sites, sign up for one today!!!

Mistake #2: Assume That Because an Experience is Meaningful to You, It is Going to Be Meaningful to Charlie and His Aunt. . .Because It Won't Be

I realize this sounds horribly negative and pessimistic and, perhaps more so, downright cynical. It is and it isn't. One of the dirtiest words in publishing is "Memoir." I would say that the majority of proposals that appear in my inbox are for memoirs or autobiographies that chronicle not-all-that-uncommon experiences we all share in our daily lives. I would also say that I reject 99.999% of them, not because they are badly written or don't contain the ability to educate and uplift the potential reader. I reject most memoirs because the majority of them aren't written by celebrities, and even then a memoir can be a really tough sell. This gets back to the point I made above—unless a reader or a publisher or an agent has heard of you, they probably aren't going to be interested in reading your life story, regardless of how deeply the experiences you relate have impacted you. This is perhaps one of the most brutal realities I've had to share with potential clients. An author's platform is always important, but it's even more important when pitching a memoir.

As you are considering the story you want to tell, ask yourself: 1) Has my story been told before? Chances are, in some form or another, it probably has. It then benefits you to consider how your story is better and/or different from what is already out there. Do your research. Spend some time browsing the shelves in your book or idea's category. How can you bring something unique to your story that hasn't been presented or shared in the same way before? And 2) Who is your target audience? It is so important to be clear on this, just as it is equally important to understand that your book isn't going to appeal to everyone. Whittle down your proposed target audience and write your book to that market. It's okay to have a secondary or even tertiary market in mind, but for the purposes of your book, make sure you know that initial target audience like the back of your hand and tailor your idea accordingly.

Mistake #3: Assume That Your Book is for Everyone

It isn't. I touched on this a bit before, but I want to go into it a little deeper because all too often I've seen authors try to convince publishers and agents in their proposal that their book is targeted to the broadest possible audience. I understand the thought behind this, but ultimately you are doing yourself (and your book) more harm than good.

Publishers want to see that your book is focused. In trying to make it all things to all readers, authors tend to lose sight of the fact that there is a specific audience to whom they should write. For example, if your book is about beekeeping, in your proposal you should say that your target audience is apiary enthusiasts. These are the people who are most likely going to be actively looking for a book on how to set up a beehive. Once you've targeted this set of the population, make sure you get to know the market. Publishers (and agents, for that matter) love statistics. They want to see, in numeric terms, the size of this particular demographic in addition to its book-buying and general spending habits. This information helps publishers determine how they're going to market/promote your book, the amount of dollars they should budget on behalf of this, and —quite frankly—whether the target market can support another book on this topic.

Also, you have to think about where your book is going to be shelved in a bookstore. Booksellers rely on the information a publisher provides them about a book's target audience. It informs the bookseller where to shelve the book. If, on the back cover, they see more than one category listing, chances are your book won't be shelved where—in this case—apiarists are most likely to look for a book on the subject. Therefore, because you weren't specific enough in your initial audience breakdown, your book may become difficult to find which serves no one's benefit, least of all your own.

When working with authors on their proposals, I always insist they list the Primary Audience first, followed by a Secondary and sometimes Tertiary audience. It's good to demonstrate that your book has the potential for mass appeal; however, typically the focus should be on that first category of readers. By doing so, you are showing that you know your potential audience, that you've done your research, and that you have a realistic perspective.

Mistake #4: Try to Publish Without an Agent

I have a caveat to this—if you're planning to self-publish, you really don't need an agent. However, if you don't have the cash to fund your publishing endeavor yourself or you have dreams of being published by the likes of a Random House or a St. Martin's Press...you need an agent.

An agent serves a number of roles, though not all of them are necessarily publishing-related, but I'll get to that another time. Agents are the bridge between the author and the publisher. From a publisher's perspective, the literary agent serves as a filter, another set of eyes, quality control. Editors receive thousands of proposals, query letters, and manuscripts every day. The ones that come from an author directly more often than not end up on what's called The Slush Pile where they sit and sit and sit, unread and unloved, until a college intern or an assistant rather perfunctorily sifts through it looking for addresses to which to send the impersonal rejection letter.

If a proposal or manuscript comes from an agent, however, chances are greater that the editor/publisher is familiar with the agent, and even the project itself, and is more likely to respond with interest or a polite "This just isn't right for my list at this time." An agent is also crucial in being able to help you target the right editor or publisher for your submission. I mentioned before the importance of being specific in choosing your target audience. This is also true in targeting the appropriate editor. An agent has the resources to be able to see what subjects certain editors are currently acquiring. This information helps them make sure your proposal is going to the editor most interested in your book's topic.

Further, an agent is able to help look out for your best interests when it comes to offer and contract negotiations. As with anything legally-oriented, publishing contracts are notorious for being difficult for the average person to understand. As an author, you want to make sure you have someone on your team looking for any loopholes or clauses that might cause confusion or difficulty down the road. A publisher also prefers dealing with the contractual stuff through another publishing professional. It saves them time from having to explain clause-by-clause the various terms of any publishing agreement. That's the agent's job.

And finally, an agent handles all of the financial aspects involved in getting your book published: from the advance and subsequent royalty payments to sub-rights and other nontraditional distribution deals. Believe me, you will want an agent to help you make sense of royalty statements.

Like I said at the top of this column, if you intend to launch your career as a published author by self-publishing, an agent isn't a necessity. However, like the majority of writers out there who dream of big distribution numbers and the prestige of signing with a well-known house, an agent is instrumental in getting you there.

Mistake #5: Become Too Attached to a Title

Another mistake I've seen authors make is to become too attached to a particular title that they won't even consider anything else. Sure, it is important to include a catchy or insightful title (and subtitle) with your book proposal. You want to capture that literary agent's immediate attention. However, chances are that title that you've spent so much time creating and soliciting advice about from friends, family, and acquaintances won't make it past the initial publishing committee. Obviously, your book's title is going to be one of its first selling points. Because of this, publishers spend hours upon hours in meetings devoted to titling your book. Believe me, I've been there. Titling meetings are among the most boring and oftentimes frustrating experiences that any acquisitions editor or publisher has to endure. But it is a very necessary evil.

It typically works like this. Your acquisitions editor asks you to brainstorm four or five additional titles that might work. He or she then brings your list into the titling meeting, which usually consist of the publisher, the sales directors, marketing and publicity manager, your publicist assigned to your book, and often the cover design team as well. They go back and forth, hem and haw, and come up with some suggestions of their own. Your acquisitions editor then goes back to you with the title options the team has created and solicits your opinion. More often than not, the title of your published book will not be the one you had originally proposed. However, I have seen occasions where after all this work, the team agrees that the initial title will work after all and runs with it.

This can be very frustrating and very time-consuming. Remember, although the material is your own, the publisher reserves the right to make all final decisions about how your book is titled and packaged. If you are adamantly against a particular title, be able to articulate why. It is in your best interests do so without sounding too defensive. Ultimately though, everyone wants you to be happy with any decisions made about your book...including the title. Publishing is a very pseudo-collaborative process and generally, when all is said and done, things work out nicely for all parties involved.

Just remember: the title is one of the most important selling factors for your book. As frustrating as the process often is, the best thing an author can be is flexible. That way, it's a win/win situation for everyone.

Mistake #6: Ignore Deadlines

Ugh...we all have deadlines and we all find ourselves scrambling at the last minute to either complete a task or project on time or try to find ways to extend that dreaded due date. The same is true, if not more so, in publishing. Publishers have very specific dates in mind for when a manuscript needs to hit each of its respective deadlines. An entire season can hinge on whether a book is published at its scheduled time. If you, as the author, are late in getting your final edits back to your editor or if you keep soliciting outside advice on your book's title or cover design to the point where you can't make a final decision, the success of your book could truly be at stake.

Once the publishing contract has been signed, one of the first duties of your acquisitions editor is to go over the production schedule with you. Keep in mind, that there is often greater room for flexibility here than most editors will have you believe. Still, it is imperative that you turn in your work on time. As ego-bruising as it may be to admit that your book isn't the publisher's number one priority, it's true. Depending on the size of the publisher, there could be anywhere from twenty to thirty other books at various stages of the production cycle simultaneous to yours. In order to keep everything running smoothly—and to preserve your editor's sanity—it behooves you to stay on track. Or, if you know in advance that you're running behind, be sure to alert your editor sooner rather than later.

If absolutely necessary, a book may be pushed back a season...sometimes two. No one is happy about this—least of all the bookstore buyers—but it happens. A delay beyond this oftentimes, however, spells your book's doom. Book release dates are determined by a number of factors, most of which are somehow tied into the book's marketing/pr schedule. If you start missing your deadlines, the window of opportunity for your book from a sales and marketing perspective narrows exponentially. No one wants to see this happen.

So, be organized, stick to your deadlines, communicate with your editor if you anticipate a delay…and everyone should be happy.

Mistake #7: Ignore an Agent's Submission Guidelines

I don't know how many times I've seen this. Agents post submission guidelines on their websites for a reason. It is your responsibility as an author to make sure you adhere to these guidelines, whether it be for submitting a novel manuscript or a non-fiction proposal. If you don't, you are only shooting yourself in the foot and limiting your chances even further of getting picked up for representation.

With fiction, I know it's tempting to give an agent more than they request. As an author in the process of pitching his first novel to agents myself, I'm with you. Still, if an agent asks for a succinct cover letter, a 2-3-page plot synopsis and the first 5 pages of manuscript—do NOT send them 10 pages. I can almost guarantee that you are setting yourself up for rejection. Agents don't have a lot of free time to look at new material. A good agent—like a good acquisitions editor—is bombarded with dozens of proposals and manuscripts at any given time. When he or she does have time to consider new work, they are going to be attracted to something well-written of course, but almost more importantly, something that grabs their interest within the first couple of pages. If you can't do that within 5 pages, you need to work on your opener. If an agent likes what he or she reads in those first 5 pages, they will probably ask to see more.

With non-fiction, you have a bit more leeway, though not much. Make sure you pay attention to an agent's non-fiction proposal guidelines before you submit your work to them for consideration. Or, if you're not sure, feel free to email them any questions you might have. Don't call. Most agents don't like talking to writers they haven't already had some interaction with before. The important things to include in a proposal are:

1. An Overview (a couple paragraphs describing your book idea)
2. Target Market (who is the book targeted toward? We've talked about this here before.)

3. Table of Contents (it doesn't have to be carved in stone because changes happen during the writing/editorial process, but be sure to include catchy chapter headings as well as a 3-4 sentence summary of each chapter's contents.)

4. Deliverables (when do you estimate delivering the final manuscript? How many words do you estimate? Any pictures, graphs, charts, or other illustrations?)

5. Competitive Title Analysis (what's already been published on your subject, when and by whom? How is your book different and/or better than its competition? Be thorough in your research and analysis. Don't ever say your book is the only one of its kind. Agents won't be impressed. They'll just assume you were lazy and didn't do your homework.)

6. Author Bio (a couple paragraphs about yourself, your qualifications, etc.)

7. Marketing/PR Platform (what are you already doing to promote and brand yourself as an expert in the field you are writing about? What resources can you draw on to help the publisher market/promote your book once it's published? This is an essential part of any strong book proposal…and often the most difficult part to write.)

8. Sample Chapters (usually two suffices. Choose the chapters that you feel are most representative of your overall narrative.)

If you're proposal is anywhere in the 75-100 pages length, it's too long and probably won't get read. Keep proposal jam-packed with information, but you don't want to exceed 50 pages at most. My preference actually is around 30, but every project is different.

Agents may differ on some of this information but generally what I've listed above is what most are looking for. Be sure though to check the agent's website before sending them anything. Also, it's important to see how they prefer to receive proposal and manuscript submissions. Most prefer email though not necessarily as attachments. Some are old school and prefer you to send materials through snail mail. It's important that you pay attention to this. At the very least, it helps you get your foot in the door.

Mistake #8: Assume that the Author Advance is an Indication of a Publisher's Commitment to Your Book

Okay, this can be a little tricky. All authors (and agents, for that matter) love getting big advances. I mean, who doesn't want big money? The perception is often that the size of publisher's advance is an indication of the level of a publisher's commitment to your book. Here's what you need to know about advances:

An advance is not free money a publisher hands out for you to spend however or wherever you like. The best way to think about an advance is as a loan the publishing is giving you to cover any costs you might accrue during the writing of your book. I once had an author tell me that he really needed more money because his mother-in-law was about to default on her mortgage and the advance money was going to help her keep her house. Bad idea.

Advances are supposed to be proportionate to estimated sales of your book within its first eighteen months of publication. For example, if a publisher offers $45,000, that means they expect your book to earn out at least $45,000 in sales during that initial sales period. One little known fact is that if a book doesn't earn out its full advance, or the manuscript the author submits is not the manuscript the book was contracted to be, the publisher reserves the right to ask for any and all unearned portions of the advance back. Authors frequently dispute this but it is in the contract. Publishers rarely act on this, but some have and as an author, you need to be prepared for this possibility. What's the moral here? READ YOUR CONTRACT. Get to know it line-by-line. If there's anything you don't understand, make sure your agent or a trusted attorney who is knowledgeable in publishing law, goes over it with you.

Think about it though. If you get a $100,000 advance, that means you have to sell $100,000 worth of books. That's a lot of books…and potentially a lot of stress. Remember also that you won't even start to earn royalties on your book until that advance is earned out in full. This means that a lot of books never earn royalties. It can be awfully discouraging.

The sad fact—though from a business perspective it makes sense—is that publishers aren't paying out the big bucks for new books like they used to. The publishing industry was hit hard by the recession and is still struggling. As much as we might like to think that publishers publish for their sheer love of books, the cold hard fact is that publishing is a business, like any other. Publishers are in to make money. It is all about the bottom-line. And it has to be. If you think about all the money paid out to authors for books that never come close to earning out their advances, you're talking about an industry that consistently operates at a loss. It's not a good business model by anyone's perspective.

When considering offers, try to look beyond the advance. Pay attention to the royalty structure being offered, but more so, look at how creatively and proactively your publisher approaches the marketing and publicity for your book. I've sometimes advised authors to go with the publisher that may pay less up front but is really committed to marketing the heck out of your book. If the book sells, the money will follow.

Mistake #9: Act Like a Diva

I shouldn't have to say this, but I will anyway. Please, regardless of how frustrated you may become with the publishing process, do not express your frustration in any way, shape, or form that anyone can interpret as diva-like. That doesn't mean you can't have an opinion, or that you can't let your team know when you disagree with a decision being made on behalf of you or your book. The key is to maintain a diplomatic and civilized tone throughout...try to avoid swearing and—this is essential—refrain from using ALL CAPS in your email correspondence with your editor or anyone on the publishing team.

Remember, publishing is all about building relationships. Your goal should be to maintain a happy and profitable partnership with your publisher over a number of books. Also keep in mind that the publishing industry is a tiny community. Word gets around like wildfire when an author starts putting on airs and acting just generally disagreeable. You want people to like you, especially people who can help you on your path to becoming a bestselling author. I'm not saying that you have to be a pushover because there will be times where you'll need to be strong and not be afraid to put your foot down. But when you start complaining about deadlines or the number of edits you are being asked to make, or refusing to show up for publicity events, those publishing professionals who genuinely want you to succeed—because they also succeed from your success—are going to get annoyed. They are not going to want to work with you and they aren't going to put a huge effort into promoting you or your book, which is only going to upset you further.

I've worked with my share of diva authors both as an editor and as an agent. Believe me, you want your team to be excited for the day your book publishes because they want to see it do well, not because they've been counting the days until they don't have to work with you again.

Mistake #10: Beat Yourself Up if Your Book Doesn't Sell to Your Expectations

So much of publishing is based on trial and error. Books that sounded like surefire hits in the initial pitch meetings may arrive with a thud upon publication, while others that seemed kind of 'iffy' go on to major bestseller status. You just never know what's going to stick. You'll have some ups and you'll definitely have some downs. But each experience you have should be viewed as a learning opportunity. If your first book doesn't reach the bestseller list or sell 10,000 copies, there could be any number of reasons for this, but it doesn't necessarily mean that you as an author are a failure. More often than not, what contributes to a book's success is based off of what's going on in the marketplace at the time of its release. Sometimes you're lucky, and sometimes you're not. But whatever the reason, do not beat yourself up about it.

Think of it this way: your first book is what gets your foot in the door. It lays the foundation for any books you subsequently write and publish. The important thing is to get your name out there, to build and solidly establish your brand as an author, and keep the positive momentum going. Just as with anything in life, luck plays a big part. But the greater your resilience, the greater your determination.

AUTHOR BIOS

Melissa G Wilson has authored 14 books, 4 that have been on bestseller lists including Networlding, now the name of her company after her 7th book by the same name, became a #10 Amazon book for year. Melissa's passion is helping 10 authors a year write, publish and promote their books to achieve similar success. She is a frequent keynote speaker on the subject of networking and building social media platforms for thought leaders. Sign up for my blog for regular updates to this book at www.networldingblog.com. To contact me reach out at melissa@networlding.com. I would love to talk about your book project.

Jon Malysiak is the co-founder and president of the Jonathan Scott Literary Agency in Chicago, Illinois. In addition to his work as a literary agent and high school

English teacher, Jon is the author of *Birds of Dreams: A Novel* (published by Clarges Press) and the upcoming *What Would Shakespeare Do?* (published by Networlding Publishing), as well as writer of the internationally popular current affairs blog Author on the Town http://author-on-the-town.blogspot.com.

www.ingramcontent.com/pod-product-compliance
Lightning Source LLC
Chambersburg PA
CBHW070052120426
42742CB00048B/2401